Bubbles

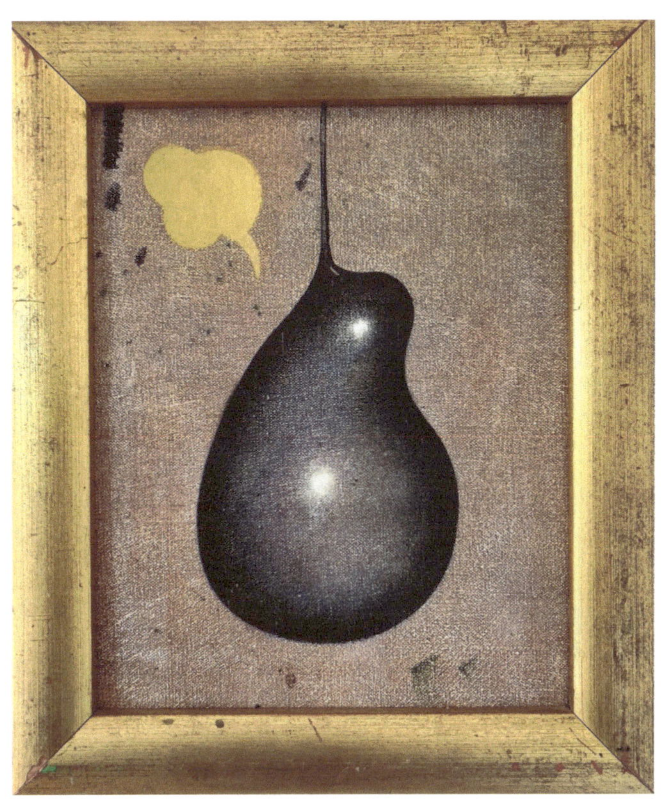

Joe Pascoe and Don Walters

BUBBLES
Joe Pascoe and Don Walters
Poems by Joe Pascoe © 2021
Artworks by Don Walters © 2021
Front Cover and Title Page: Don Walters
PORTRAIT OF A BUBBLE AND A SPEECH BUBBLE
Back Cover: Don Walters
THERE IT IS!

ISBN 978-0-6451280-7-9

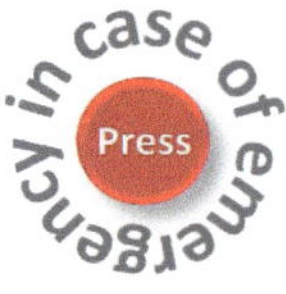

Bubbles

Book 1
On an island somewhere south of Paris

Joe Pascoe and Don Walters

Book No.   of 100

Dedication

This book is dedicated to the Bubbles in us all.

Contents

Bubbles

Book 1
On an island somewhere south of Paris

Birth

There is an island south of Paris
Where the mermaids did come to play
Making bubbles every day

They were sweet creatures
As sweet as heaven's breathe
Calling to sailors every way

In time the Bubbles grew
They knew what to do
As they blew and blew

The sun it shined
Even the moon glistened gold
Gather close, a special tale to be told

This is a special story
It's all about love
And how people breathe and believe

Enjoy every sentence
And never be scared
These beautiful Bubbles
Will lead you to a land ahead.

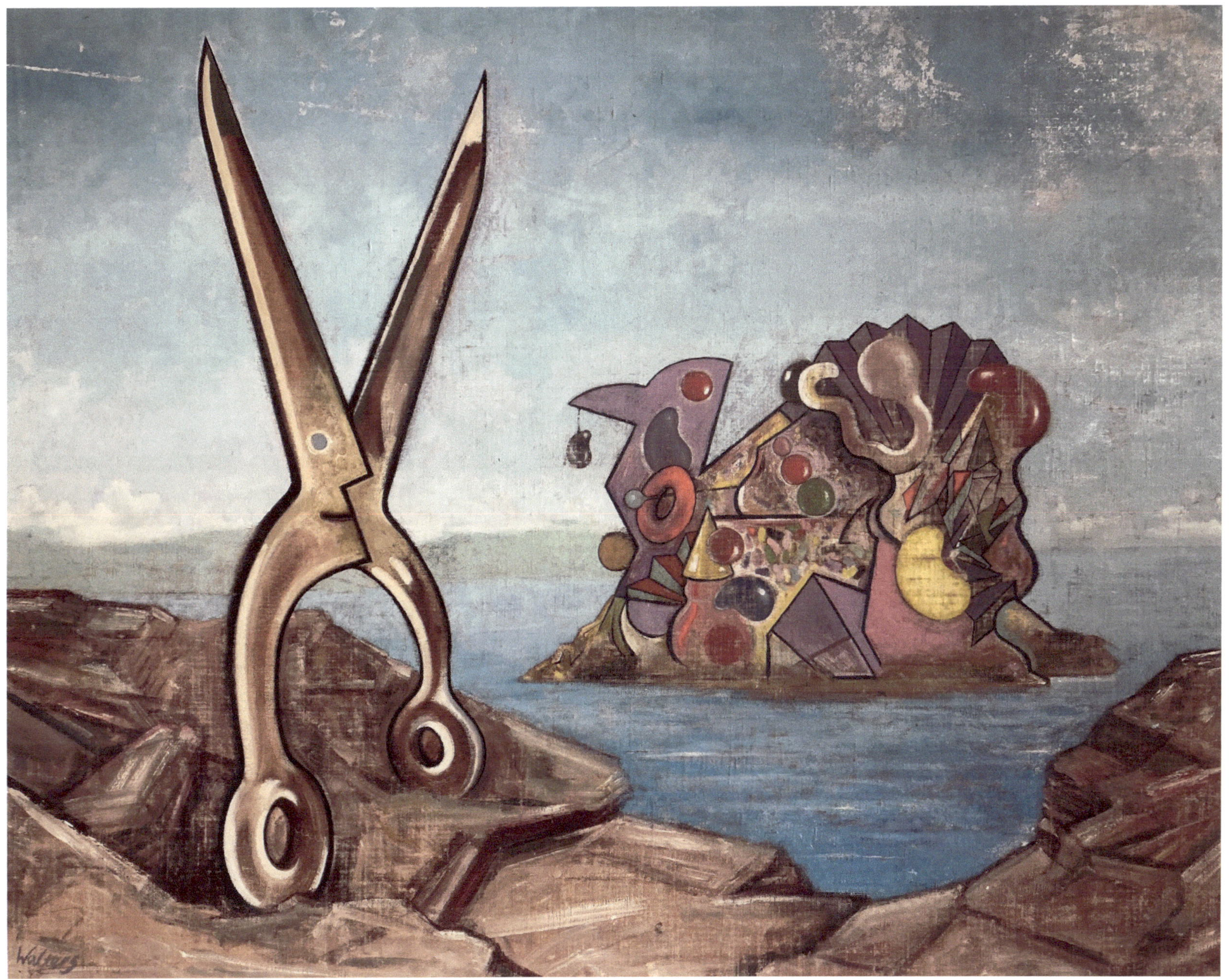

Walters

Somewhere south of Paris

Somewhere south of Paris
There was magic, magic everywhere
Matisse, Rousseau, Duchamp
Hanging from the trees like pears

Speckled and stinky
Flash and tamarind sharp
Loving and mysterious
The scenery did not stop

Ahh!
This is art my darling
It grows and grows
Oft times in rows
You can feel it between your toes!
The Bubbles walked on through the day
Evening and part of the night
To two wooden chairs, under a soft light

Their sighs and murmurs escaped
Between bits of fresh bread
As the local vin rouge
Went to their heads

A great day is a day shared
Our friendship is the real art
Not clever word or famous things
But the time together
Until the morning cock sings.

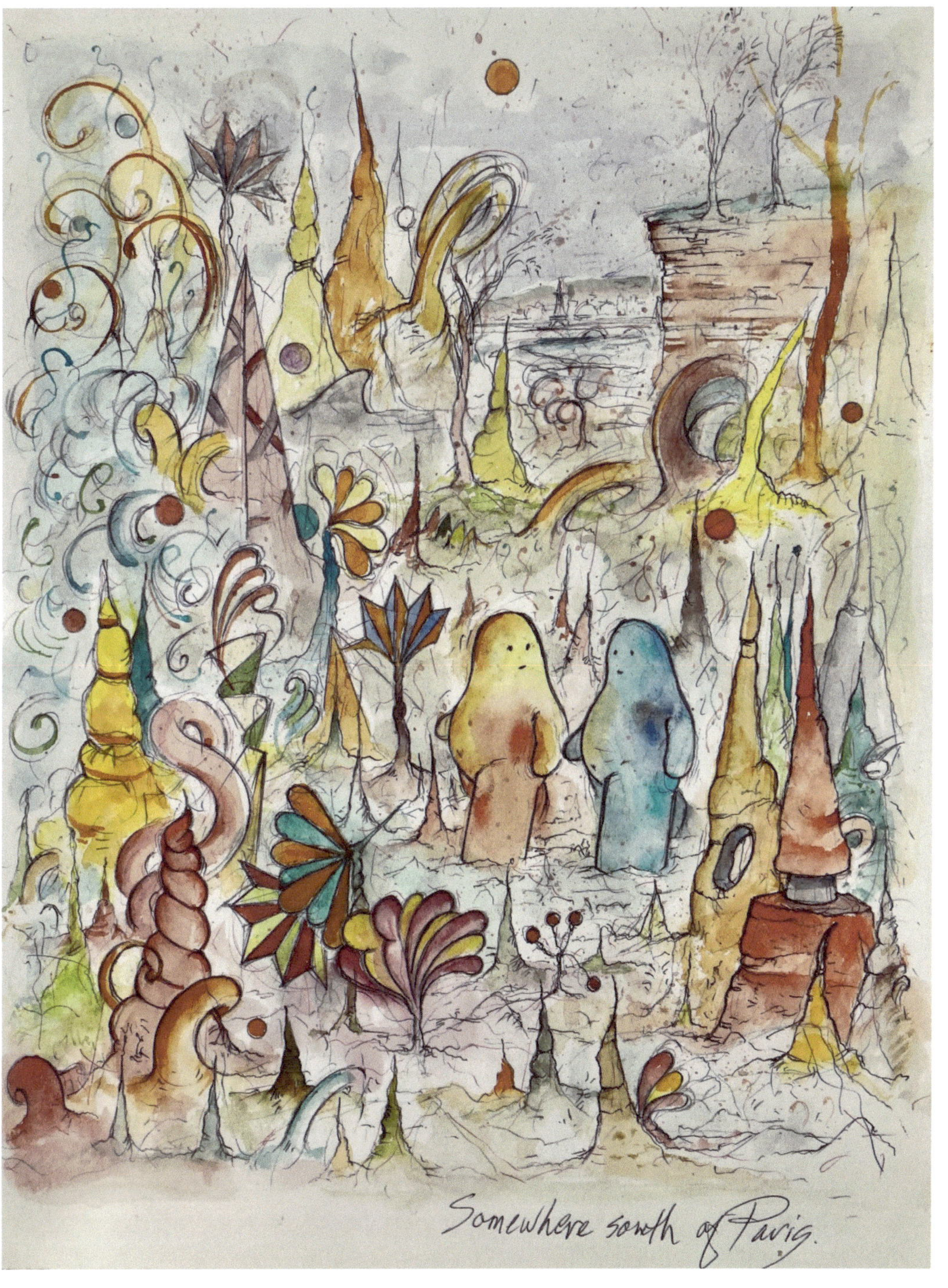

Somewhere south of Paris.

It takes all types

It takes all types
Count them, the colours
In space, floating
Descending or ascending
Arms close in, legs together
Silently en masse

I found you
Emperor penguin style
North and South Pole
Coming home
Finding your partner
Share the egg

A child comes, another
More, as many as you need
Your village, our home
Made of souls
A necklace of lives
Weaving a blanket
Ready to unfold, shake out
Lay flat, with your love
It takes all types
Too many to count
About fifty or more
One a week
For a year or more
It takes all types
But in the end
It's only you that will do.

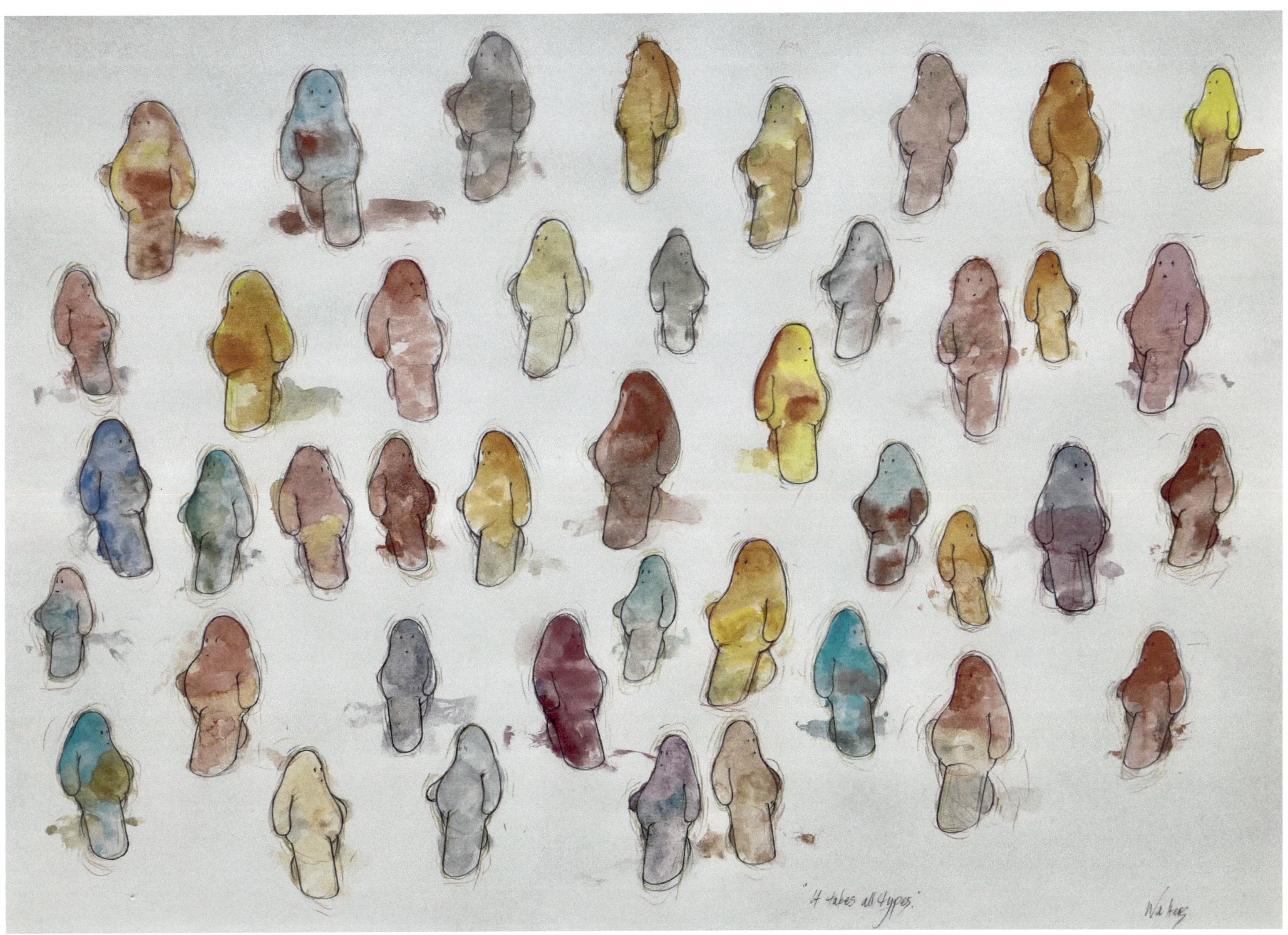

"It takes all types."

Bubbles

Bubbles
Sweet nothings
Tiny dreams
Bubbling by the millions
Everyday

You float
Take me with you
Silent magic
Colour and pop
Left in the memory

When we talk
I feel it again
Our kisses
Your smiles
Lifting us
Spraying around
Abound in the sun.

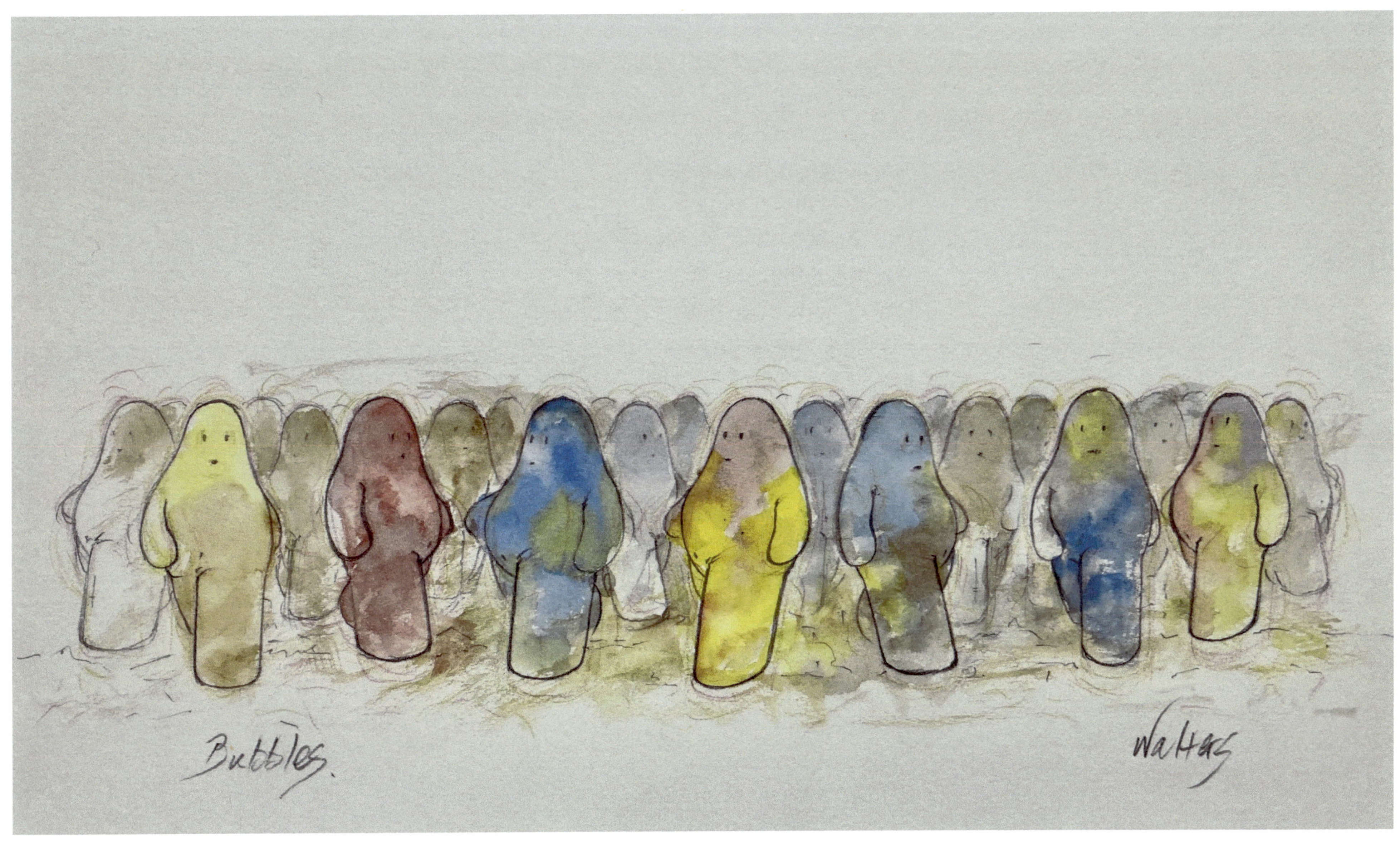

Bubbles.
Walter

Morning

Sweet sounding pedestrians
Birds in the tree
Morning it comes to all
It's a feeling of being free
Pity not the office workers
Warm enough in their coats
Day dreams filed away
Until the end of the day

Birds back to their nests
Armed with tiny twigs, plastic bits
Sharp in their beaks

We have got to hold it together
Wars and bushfires at bay
I don't want to say the word
But pray

There is always plenty of chaos
Letters tumbling, falling, crashing
Pick them up
Respect their place
Put them on the page.

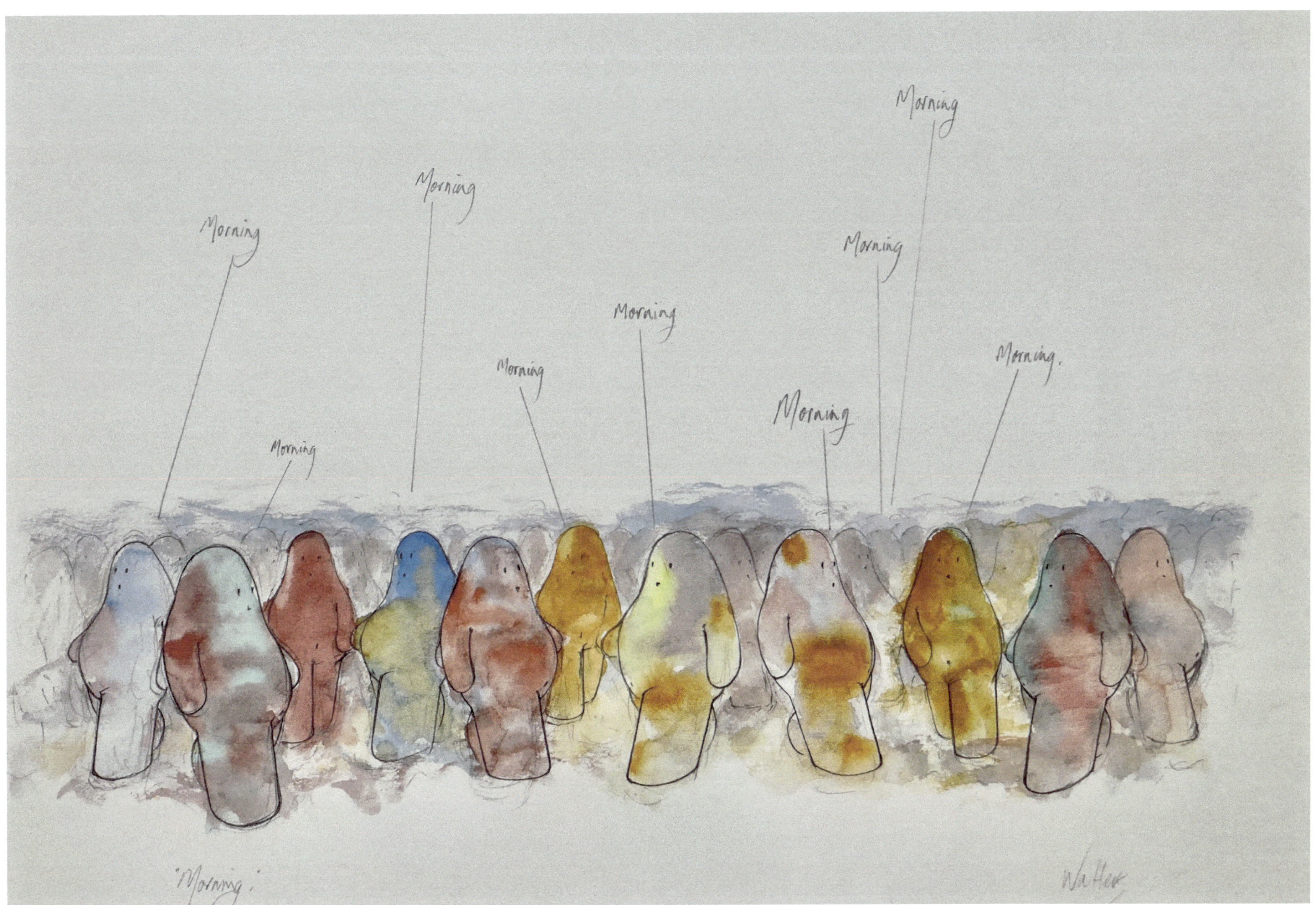

Morning
Morning
Morning
Morning
Morning
Morning
Morning
Morning
Morning
Morning
"Morning."
Walker

We were all there, but I couldn't see Ian

A gap
Strange
We were all there
But I couldn't see Ian

A moment ago
We were walking
I swear

It seems impossible
I thought I saw his shadow
Heard his voice

Picture him
Believe it's true
Gone

The gap broadens
It's everywhere
Surely, he was here

Am I wrong?
Did I dream him?
I feel cold, empty

Shall I speak?

Call his name
Reach out in vain

Expose my loss
Question everything
When did he go?

Am I here, really?
My loss is too much
That's why I stay quiet.

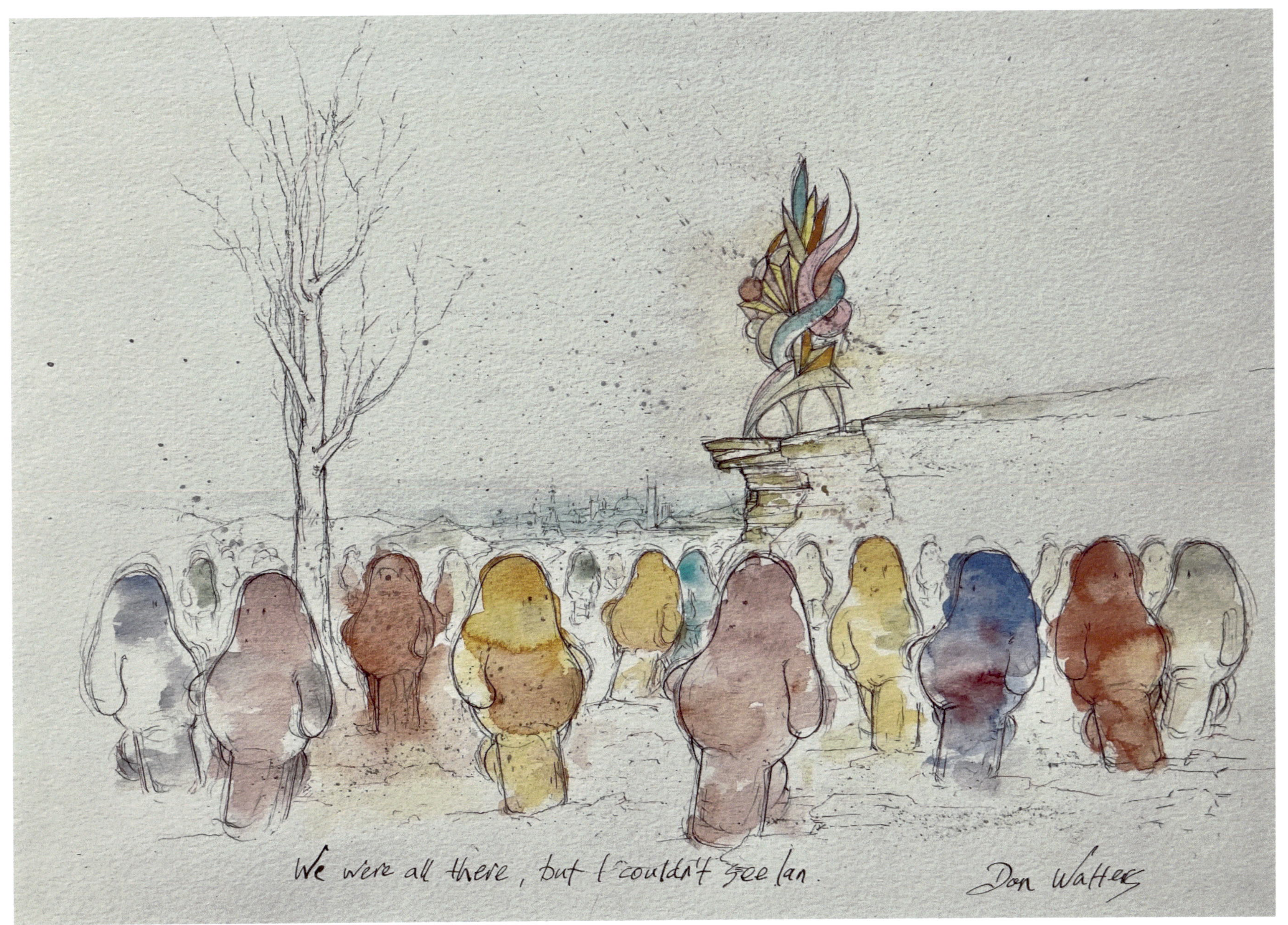

We were all there, but I couldn't see Ian.

Don Watters

I was surprised to hear my name called

Hey, Bubble Bum!
This guy knows me
I thought
Primary school, some forgotten corner?

Reassuring in its way
The essential me
Pinned in the air

A simple phrase
Convincing
Without hubris, inverted pride
Shy and friendly
You can't escape the past

I say hello
Damien, Leon?
Names from then

Suburbs and schools ago
Marriages, mistakes
Are they in my eyes?

Health check, wealth check
30 seconds allocated
Where once it was days
He wants nothing
Just emotion
An easy smile, five minutes
Not my shoulder
Quick tilt
Of the head, not the pinball machine
No one even smokes

Not anymore.

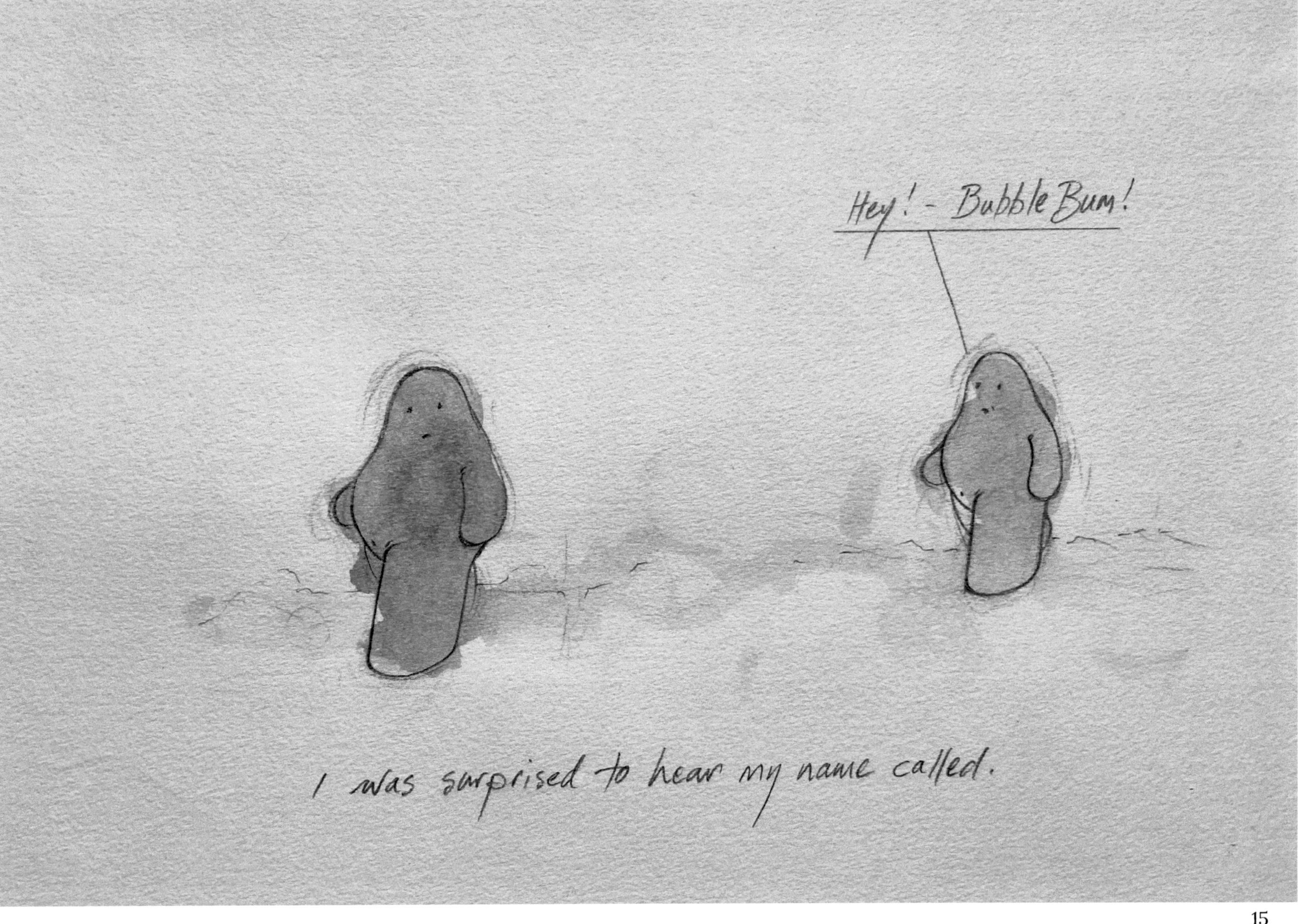

I was surprised to hear my name called.

Lost are ya, buddy?

Lost are ya buddy?
Time going slow
Colour fading away

Feeling the warmth
Feeling the pride
Just being by your side

If you can, lend a hand
Be nice, be gentle
You can jump too, holla!

Them school days are gone
Work getting slight

Ya gotta love somebody
My mum did say
We all cry in our way

Friends in the waves
On the beach, in the library
Buy a train ticket to life

Take care, don't fight

Ya still lost buddy?
Say hello
Let yourself glow
It's in the crowd, y'all get to
now.

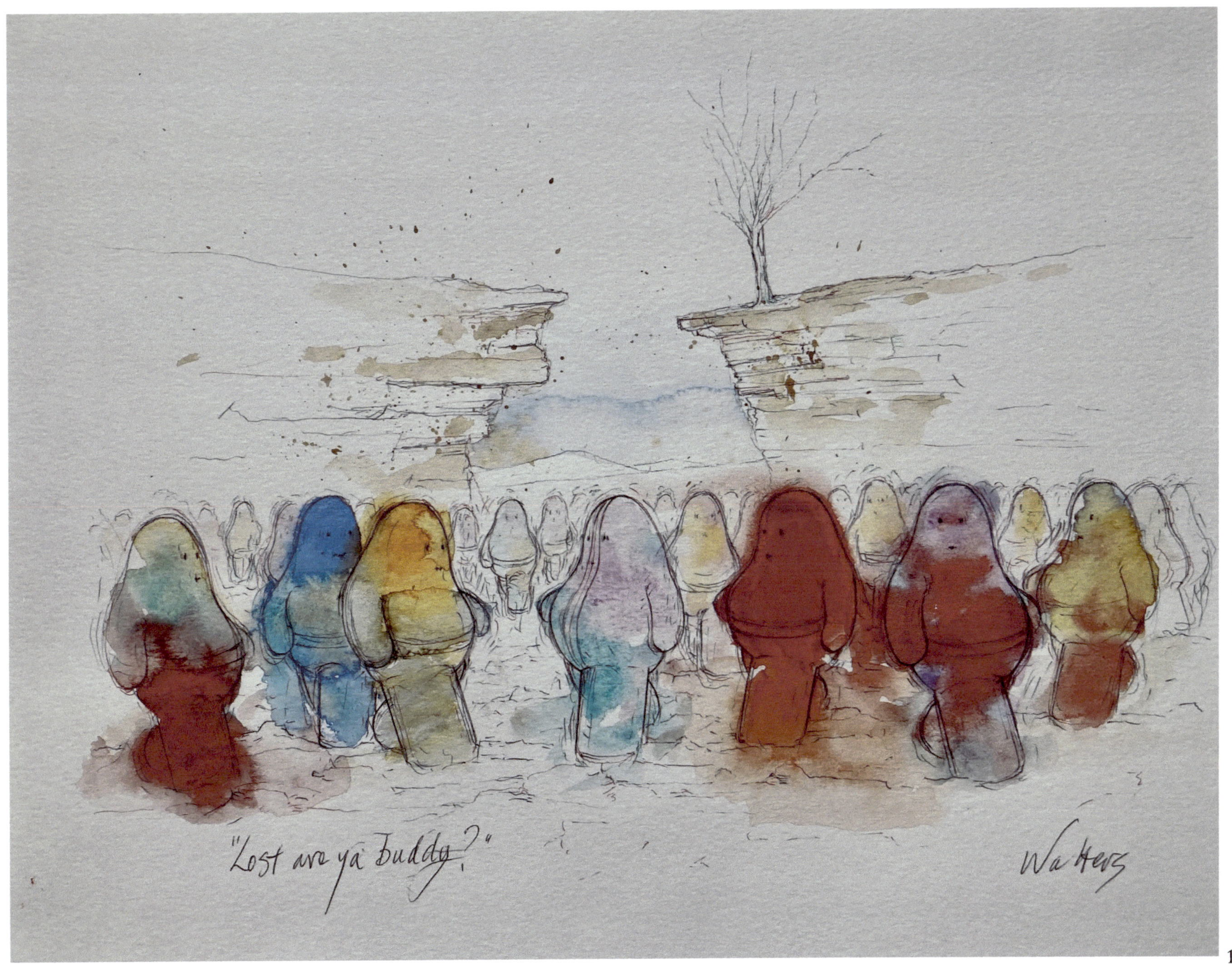

"Lost are ya buddy?"

Walters

You and me and someone else

You and me and someone else
We feel through space
Our thoughts within
Our emotions raging, paths crossing
Trying not to lose
Our hearts, our loyalties

The other, the else
Parts of the social atom
Burning, cooling
Molecular in structure
Joined in the mind
Or leaving us alone

A future
A past
Too much to say
Words will only slow you down
Better to move
Out and away

I remember you
You don't know me
My binary partner
We spin together
Please don't make me the other
Someone 'else'
A distant nova.

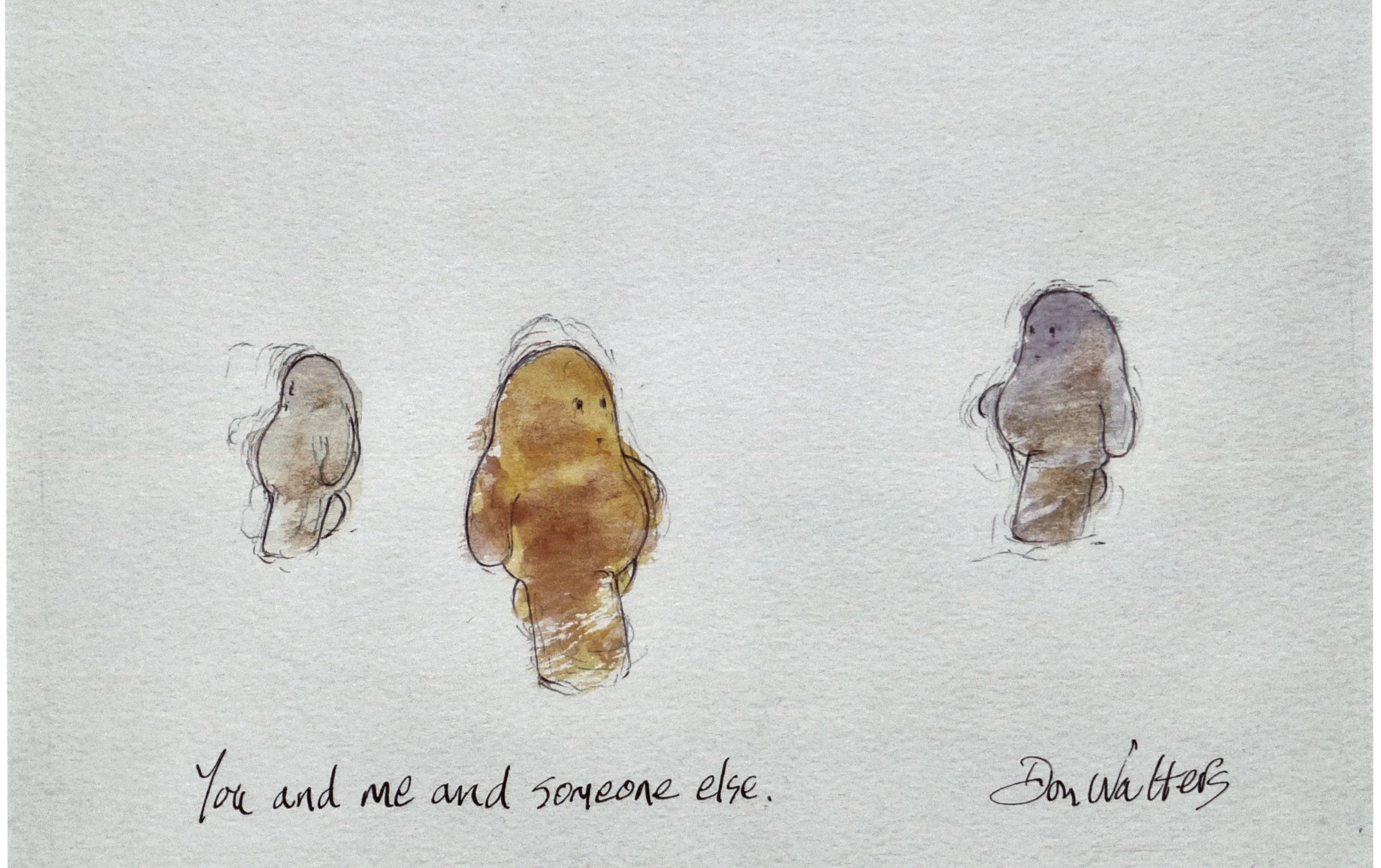

You and me and someone else.

Don Walters

I thought I'd find you here

I thought I'd find you here
In the embrace of my memory
Remembering you

In warm times we talked
Held hands and laughed
That's mostly gone

A butterfly
You can't capture it
Just watch for a moment

So I come looking
To say what words I can
But you float away

I thought I'd find you here
Sort of waiting, sort of not
In a moment, we will change.

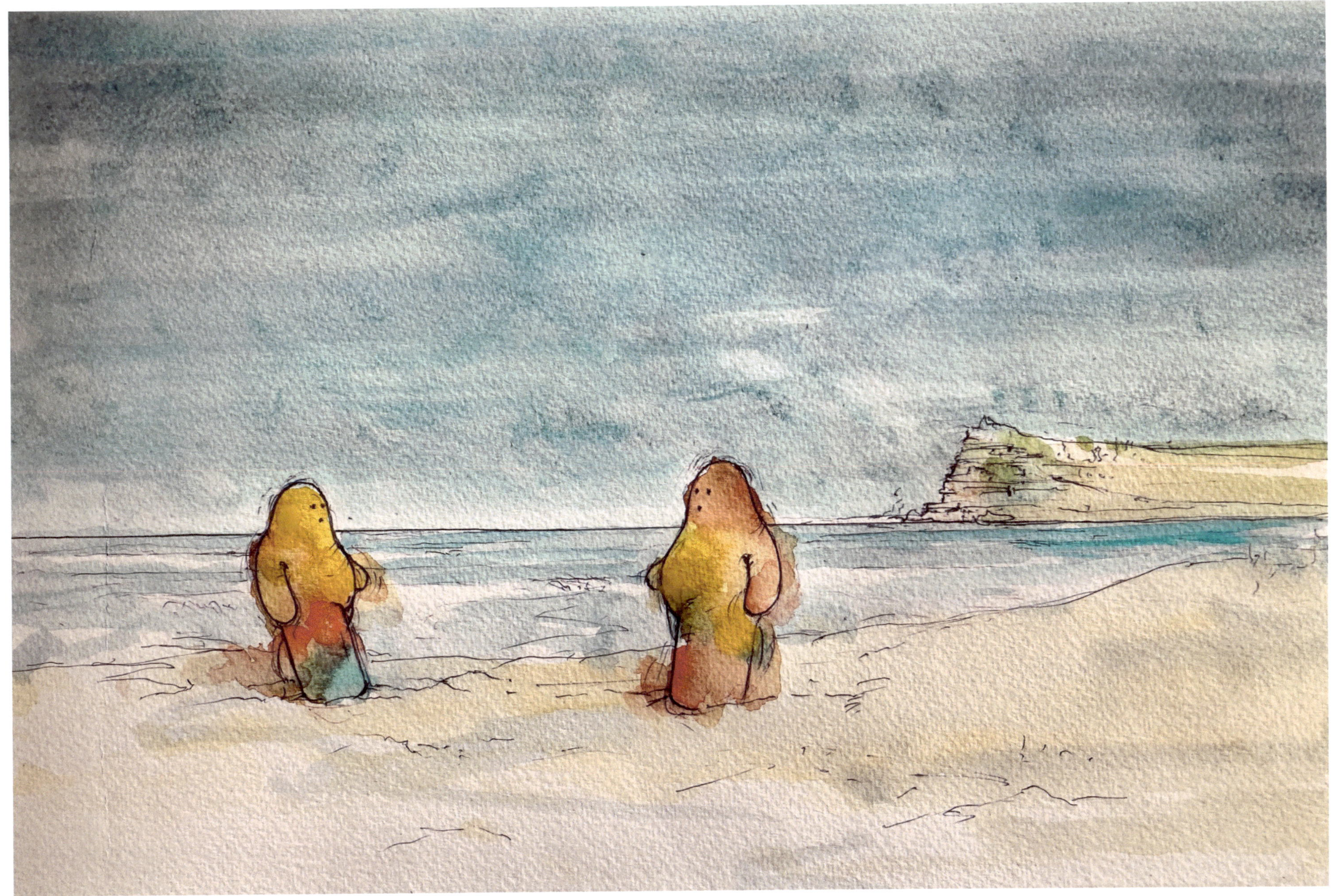

It didn't matter where they went—they were constantly followed by rain

It didn't matter where they went
They were constantly followed by rain
Was it them, was it the rain?
It's pain so plain
History's remorse, a child lost?
Their guilt, their shame

We watched them shuffle
It didn't seem to change
We hoped they were safe
And all things must change

Their lives went on
Bleak and wet
Watching for growth, on they went

It was a fate, not a curse
It could be put to use
I sometimes felt sorry
But spoke little
Did I make it worse?

Would it pass?
If they dared to dream
And so it was
On days that were very wet
They held hands
Trying to forget.

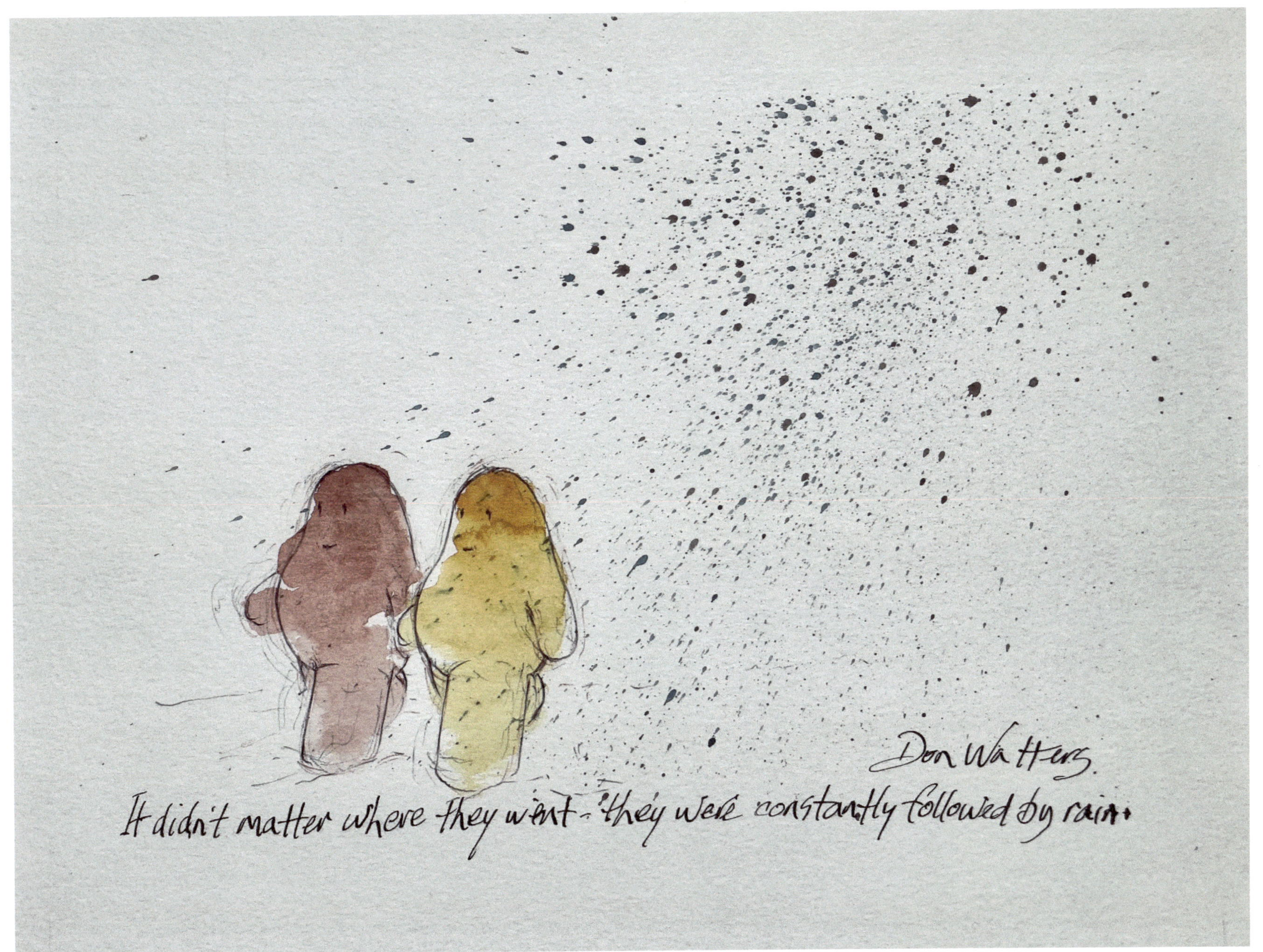

It didn't matter where they went - they were constantly followed by rain.

Don Watters.

Distracted

Glorious burning bush
hot and wild
I stand transfixed

Taught to believe
A fiery miracle

Strong and alone
You are a beacon
I come to you
Feeling my eyelids
Lips tighten
Mind combusting

Seeking redemption
I believe

No flame more beautiful
The sound of your crackling
Smokeless yet perfumed
Blessing the hill

I don't need a god
It's freewill I want
To guide me, give me grace
Glow upon my face.

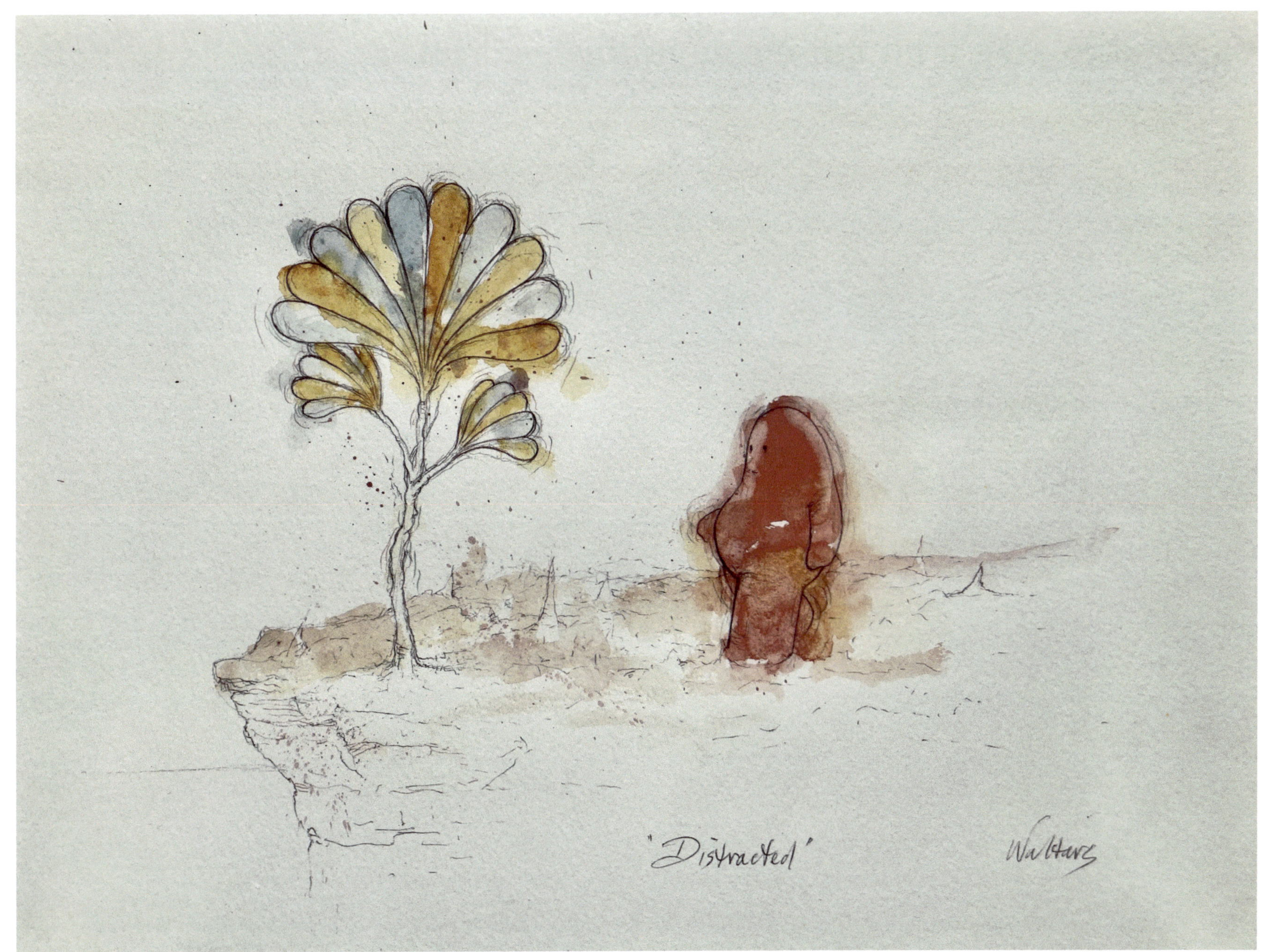

"Distracted"
Walters

You need to take a bit more care in this next bit

You see that land ahead?
It's the land of don't, where
Doubters stand
People without leaves
Or flowers or perfumes
Those who stay very quiet
Never swaying or helping
Something may have hurt them
You may never know
Step carefully through the thicket
Avoid being caught

You need to believe
In yourself, your ideas
However you see it

Be a carpenter, if you wish
An artist even
A fine school teacher
Whatever fits you right

But for me
Don't be
A thorny stick
In a salty sea.

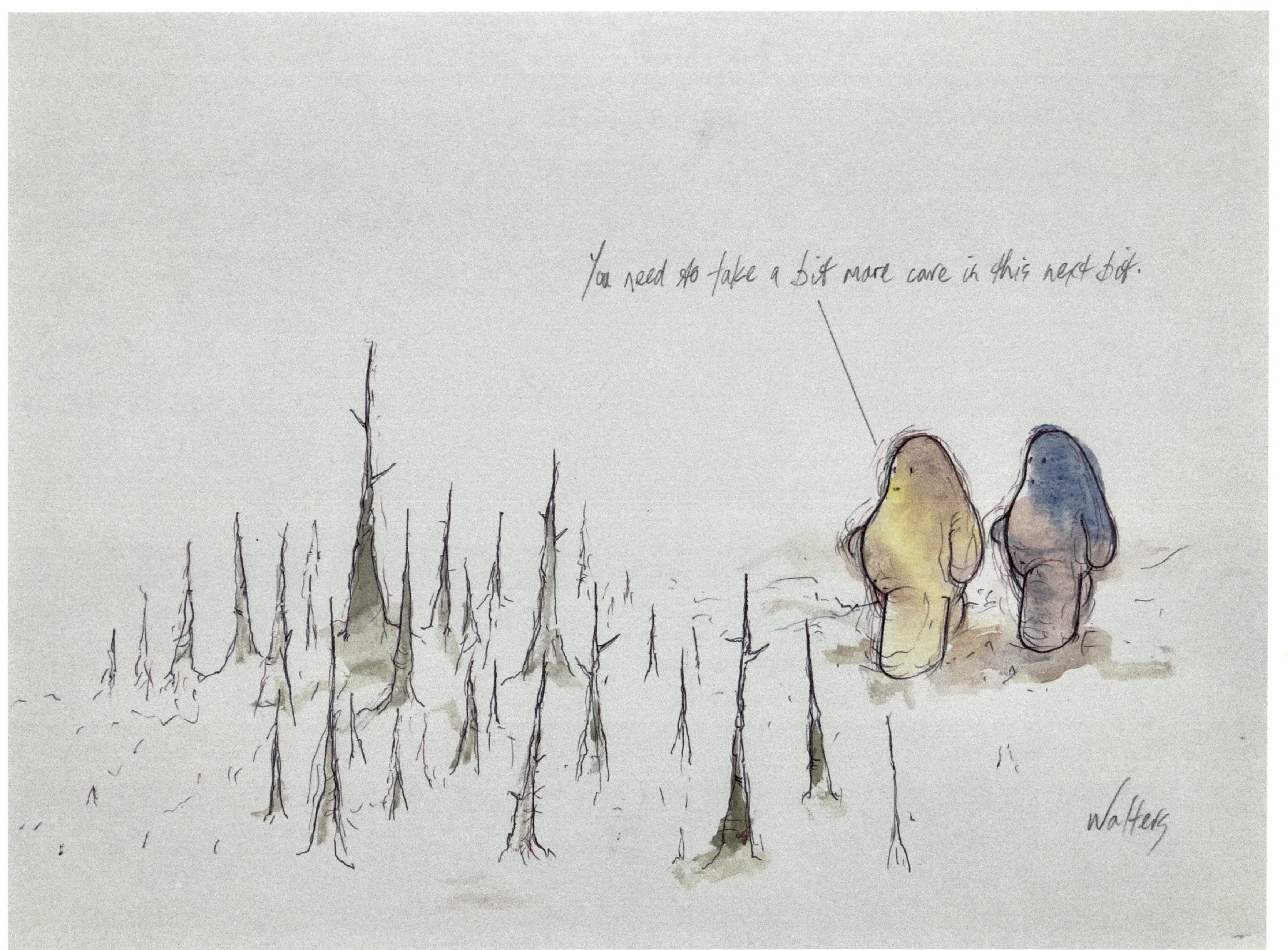
You need to take a bit more care in this next bit.

The Messiah

The Messiah
Our cookie cutter god
You divide us, we made you
And then forgot

We are in a line
Protected and layered
From unbelief to belief, we need you

We pray
You stand tall, no shadow
Yet shiny somehow

Our songs rejoice
We love the present, fearing all
A precious strand

From our mother
To mother's end
A charred voice of truth
Messiah

Let our message come
If you dare
For those that care
You need to be there.

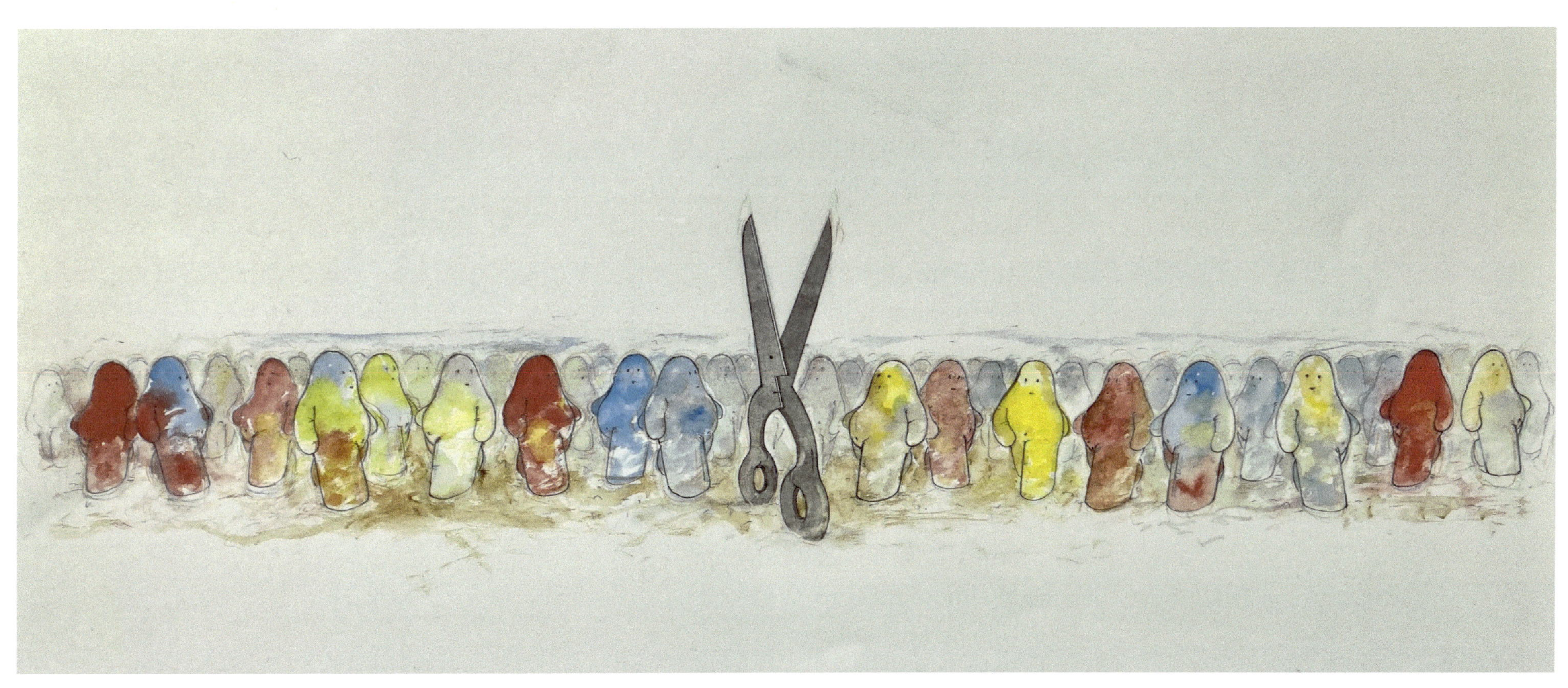

29

He's with me—OK!

Menacing man
He's with me!
You are sharp and nasty
I am solid and real
You are a nightmare
Scaring me still

But he is with me
And I am with him
Brother and sister together
Not a monster of the mind
All history has taught us
Greater is the good
Love is the precursor
Not evil or ego

Somehow the herd can split
In a moment turn
Unleashing a demon
One which I prefer to spurn

I say it again
It makes us brave
He's with me—OK!
Return to your dark cave.

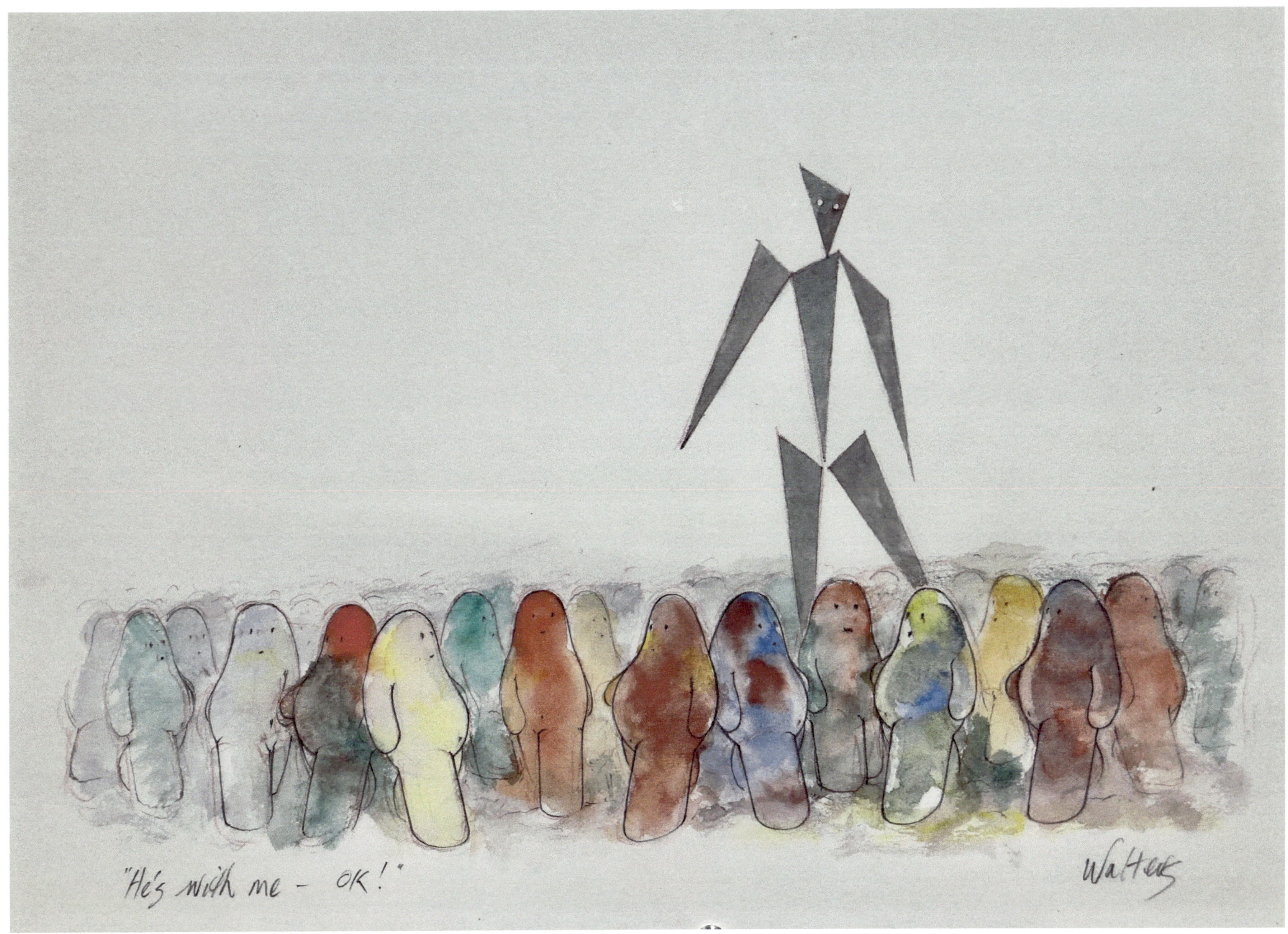

"He's with me – OK!"
Walters

I was probably the only one who saw his bad side

There's a demon in my mind
Messing me, making me unkind
Bursting a bubble
Making people disappear

I looked around
Heard the snip
Silver scissors, causing grief

I fought it well
Triggering my hate
Something is wrong, this isn't me
Am I too late?

I saw you're evil
Felt its tug
The mob was taken
They went for a swim
Gone glug gone
It's your time, worthless one
Be gone demon go.

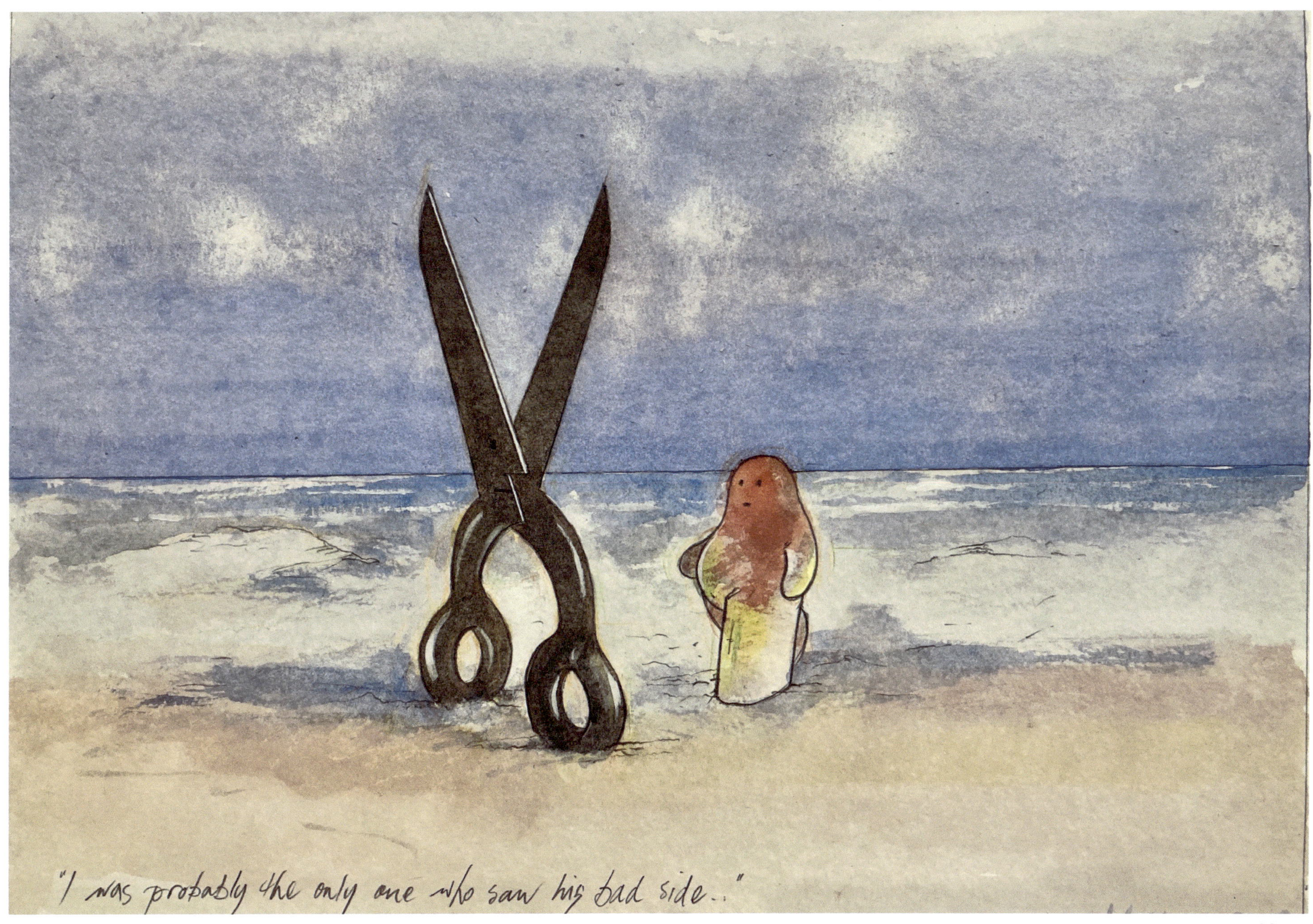

"I was probably the only one who saw his bad side.."

Coming home

Is that you god?
Coming home
Living amongst men and women
How did you go?

Did they have space?
Let you into their homes
Or sleep out
In the snow, chilly autumn

You have gone four seasons
That time on the beach
Summer, I felt annoyed

Your first autumn, like now
It probably mellowed
In autumn people don't pray
But feel the earth
Everyone is a spirit
Joined

I find winter good for death
Your business, I know

Was it good, did you help?
Snipping their souls
Away from the body
Were you careful?
A noble task

Budding springtime
Weeds and flowers
Little lambs, birds in the morning
New birth
And death feels wrong

Thus it's turned to summer again
What did you learn god?
Your handsome shape
Decisive, on the move
Are you less judgmental?
Found new ways to be wise
Dear god, can you share?
Powerful or not
Many of us still need a charm
One to hold in the palm
Safe in god's hand.

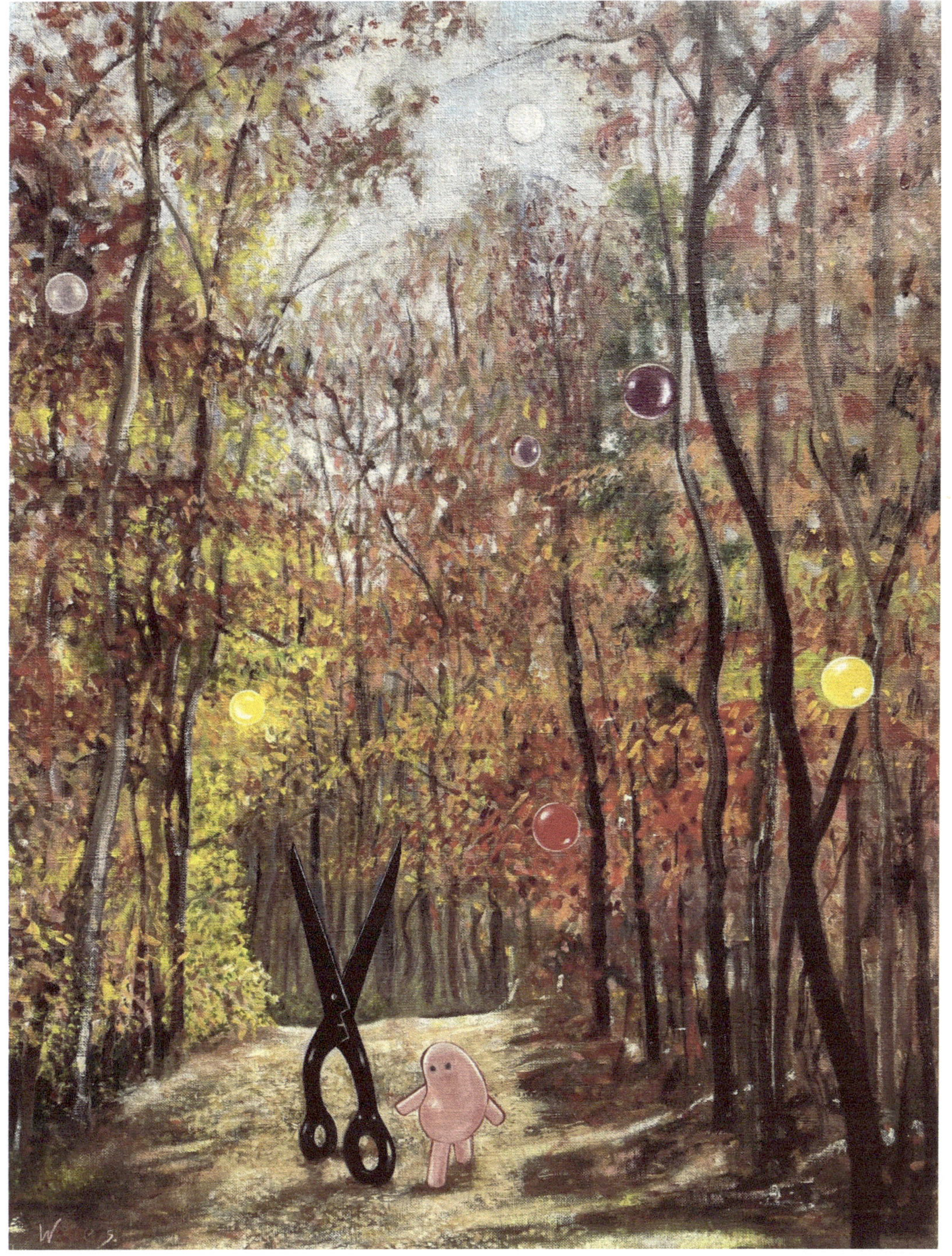

I counted six of them, but, there may have been more— it all happened so quickly

Like days in a week
I couldn't think of them all at once
Or maybe I could
Too hard to tell

Fear in me
Calm in them
Shoulder to shoulder
A schoolyard
A bag, potatoes
Ready to roll

Lame
I stood
I counted on my hand
Something to do
I'm just a guy
Feeling very alone

No Clint Eastwood here
Six shooter spitting its sound

Where's Gate 7?
That way, I said
Footy fans, that's all
My anxiety had me undone

Buried racism
Springing up
My turn to sweat
Sit down, water
Take my time
My sense of time
Gone wrong

We think we know
How to be better
Talk it through
Teach your children
Though within
The wicked, old sin
Devil with a grin.

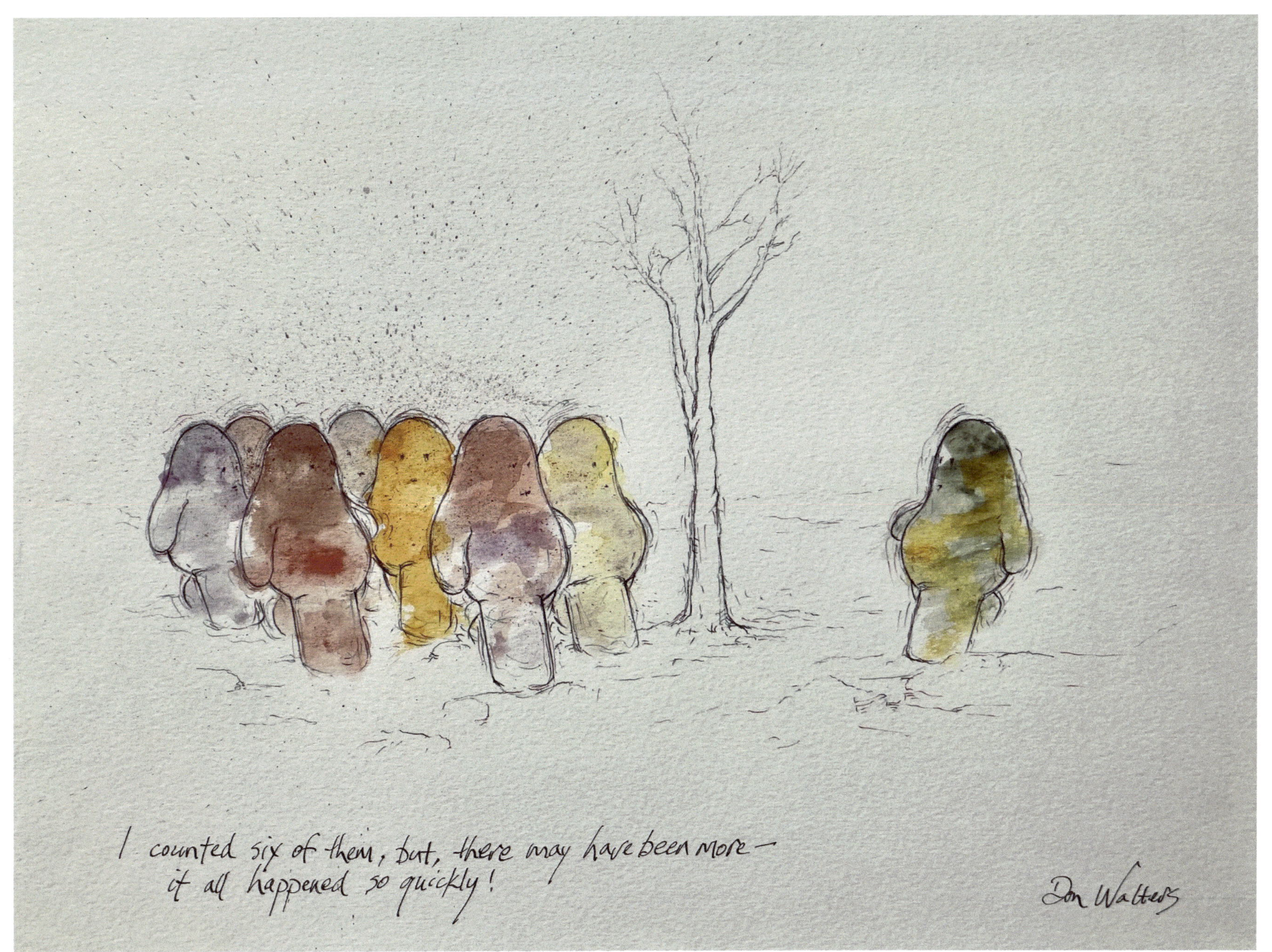

I counted six of them, but, there may have been more —
it all happened so quickly!

Don Walters

Hi, Brad, you're looking well

And so it was
On the Sunday morning
We gathered alone
Just this family of friends

All of us aged
Finding warmth in the crowd
Dressed in autumn colours
Human leaves out for a stroll

Life's easy partners
Two legs and health considered a bonus

Sometimes one of us disappears
Lowered into the ground
Or given a tune-up to motor on

We love Brad
He puts up with our Andy Warhol jokes
Reverses it, flirting lightly
Fitting into our group
Lingering and mingling

Autumn people, rustling
Waiting for the wind
To blow them away.

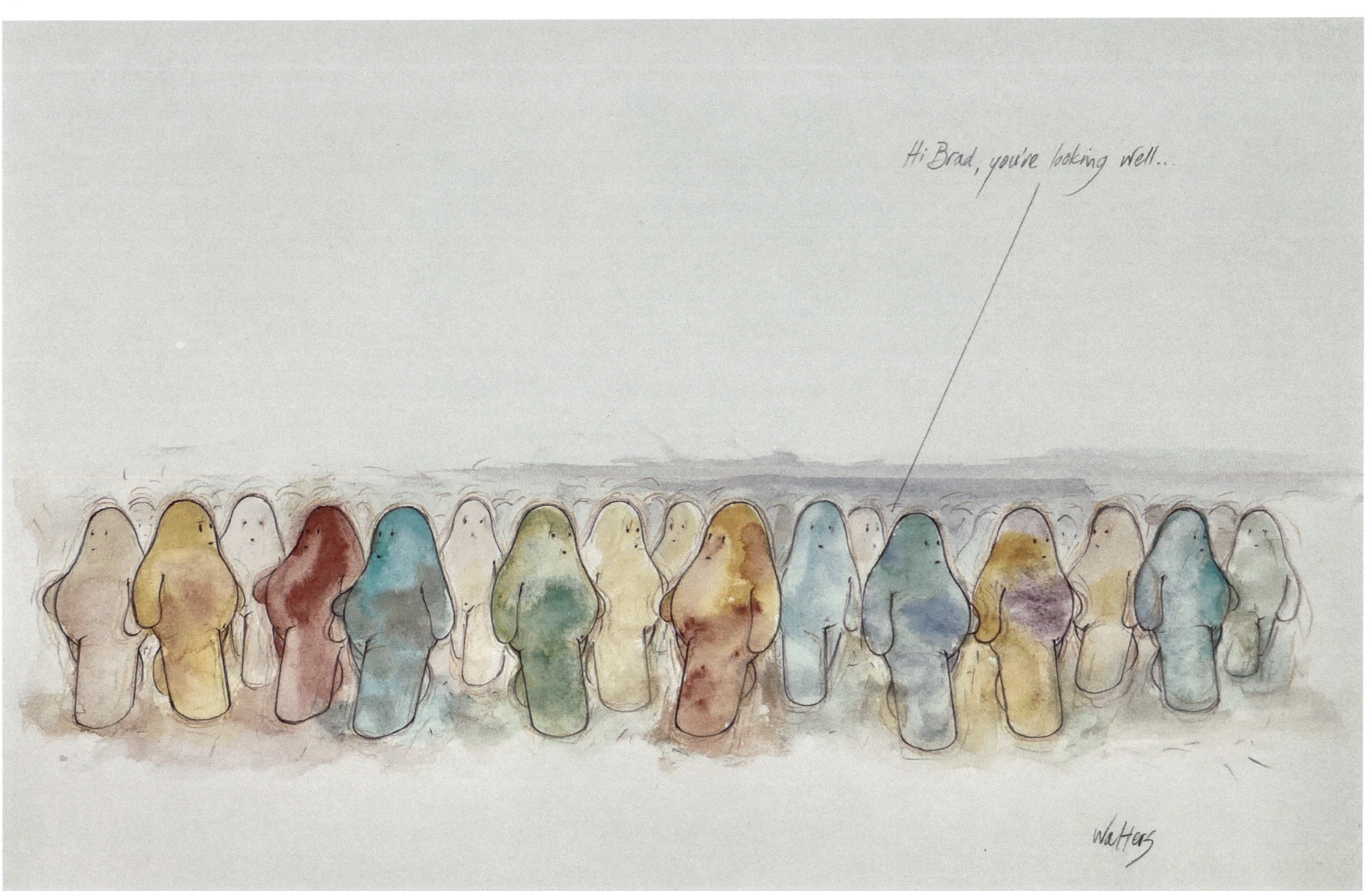

Hi Brad, you're looking well...

Walters

It seems I wasn't alone

My daughter has a new tattoo
It's wild and wraps around
Like heavy veins or vines
Snaking from hand to elbow

I'm her dad but don't stare
Her life had been in mine
Now it grows on her own
Every thought, action
Etched in my heart
Pumping strong for her

Our fears are ours
No need to pass them on
Beautiful dreams to you my child

My demons, chances, money and things
Collapsing in
Let it compress

This landscape, this life
This pair of lost socks
Are mine not hers
Don't worry about the tattoo

I always thought she would go to art school
I just didn't think it would be this cool.

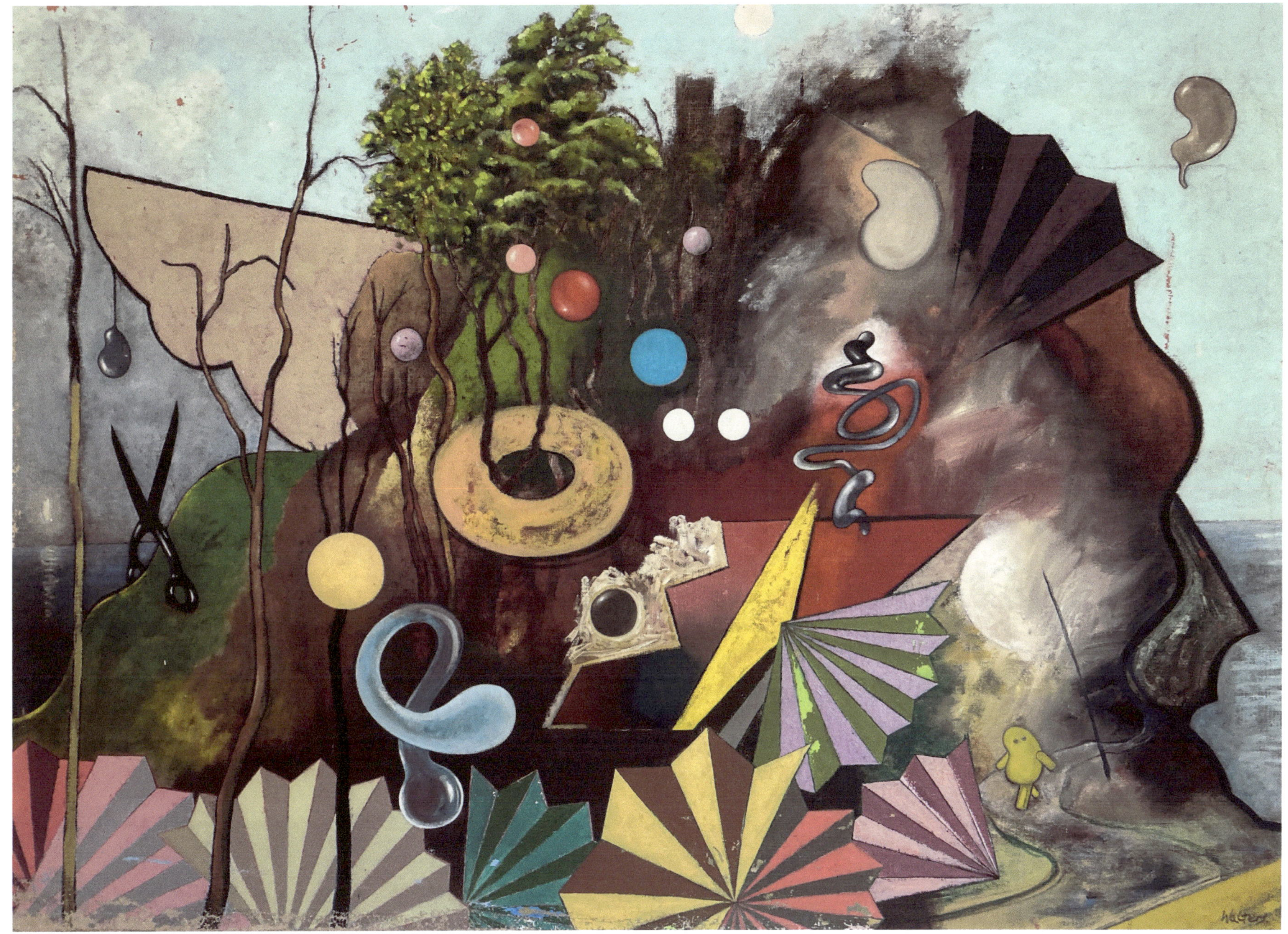

Welcome to the future

Future
Utopia
True
Unknown
Resolved
End

It's love that you will need
Planting a seed
My father said to me

A cornucopia
Strangely twisting views
All colours
Red yellow blue

Keep your eyes open wide
And your feet firmly flat
Your heart open
Mouth paused, your wallet quiet too
Son, I will always love you!

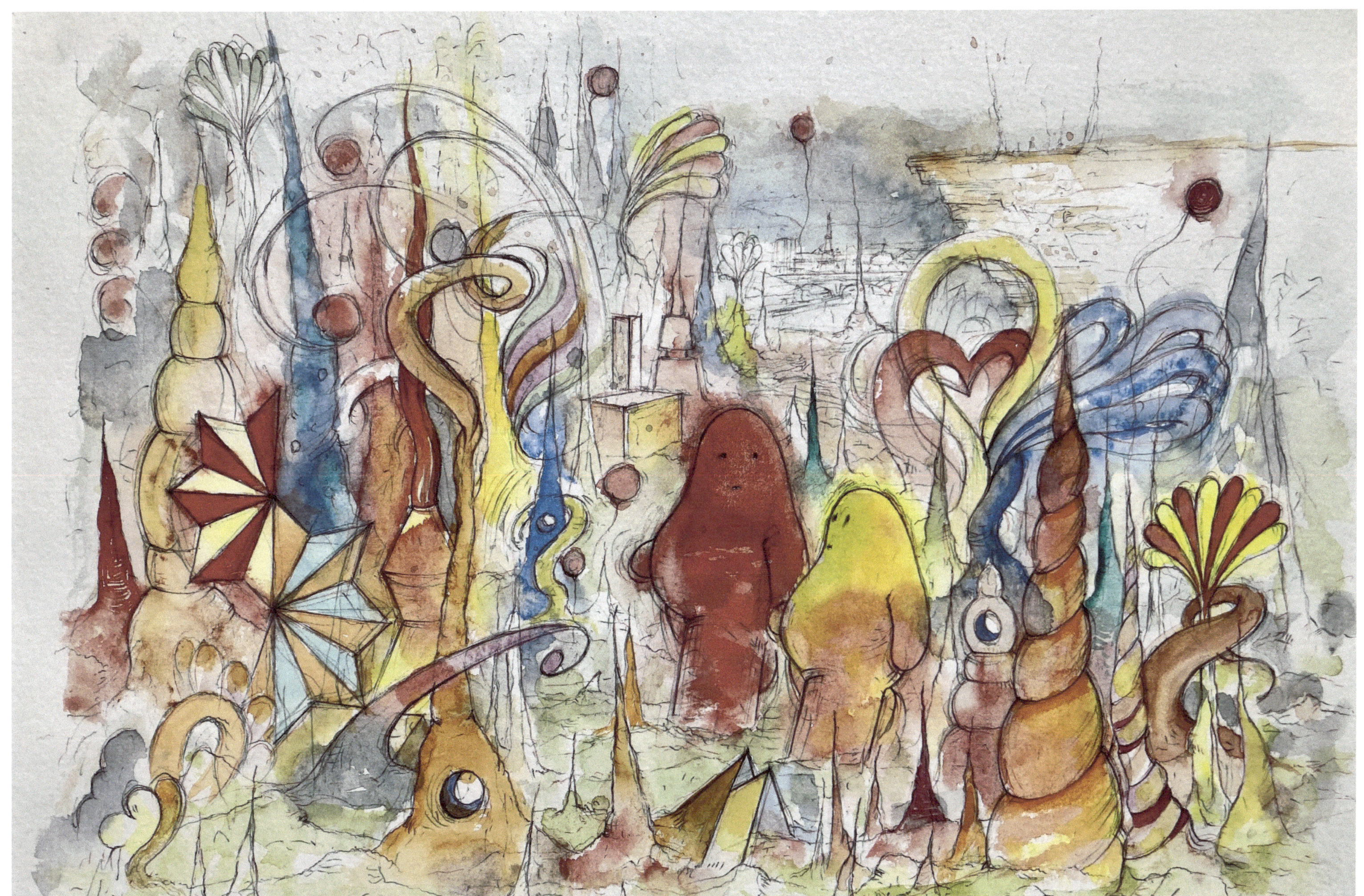

One day all of this could be yours!

Green, gold, yellow and blue
Let the widest horizons beckon you.
Remember, even the darkest day,
Black and gray,
Can help in its wiry way.
Say hello, goodbye too
Be a beautiful Bubble
Through and through!

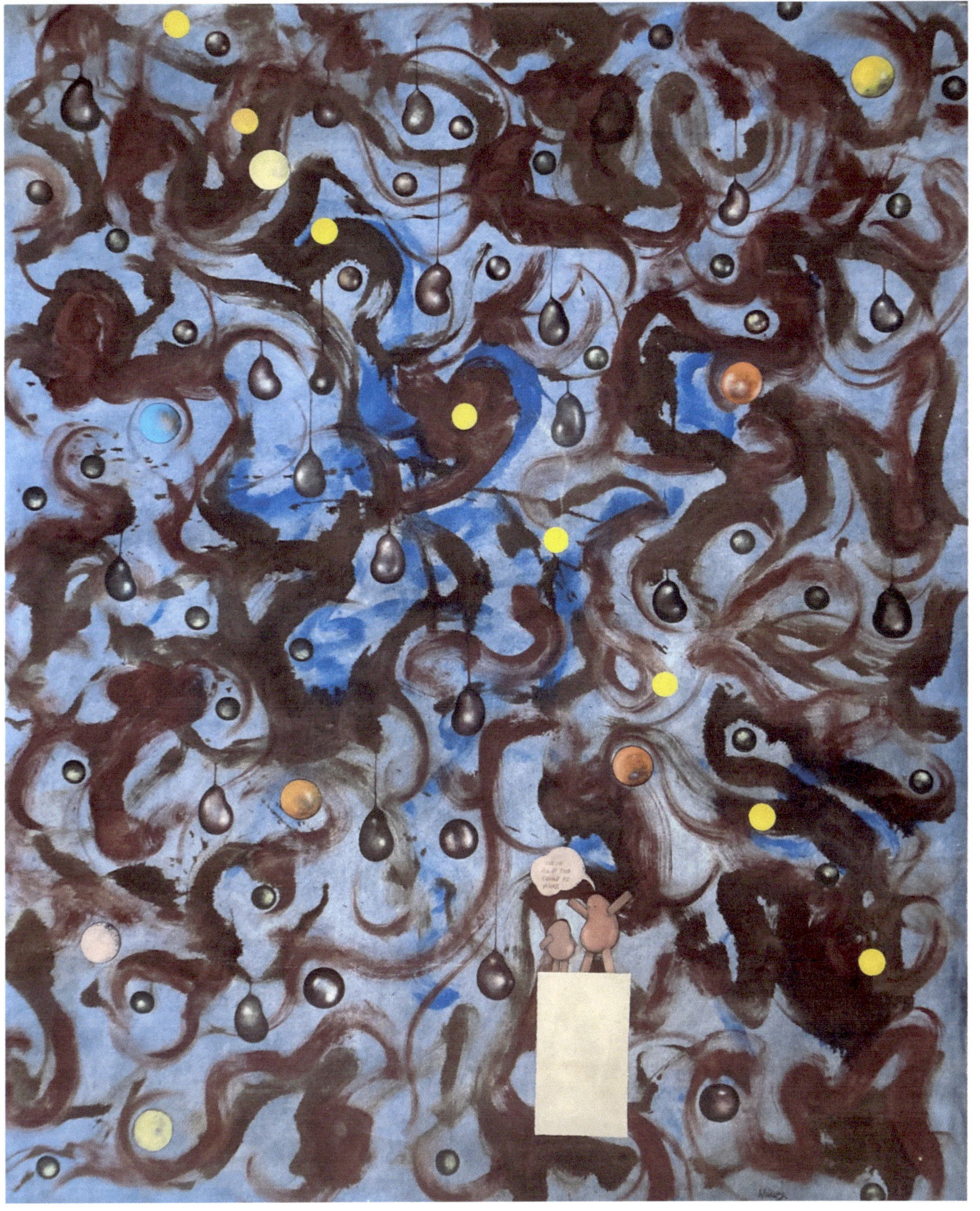

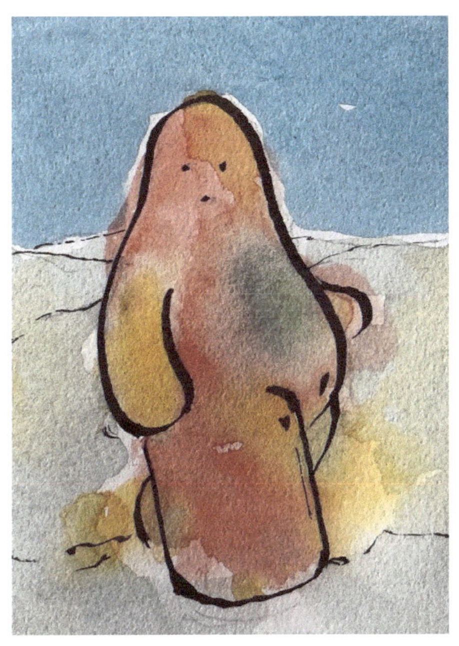

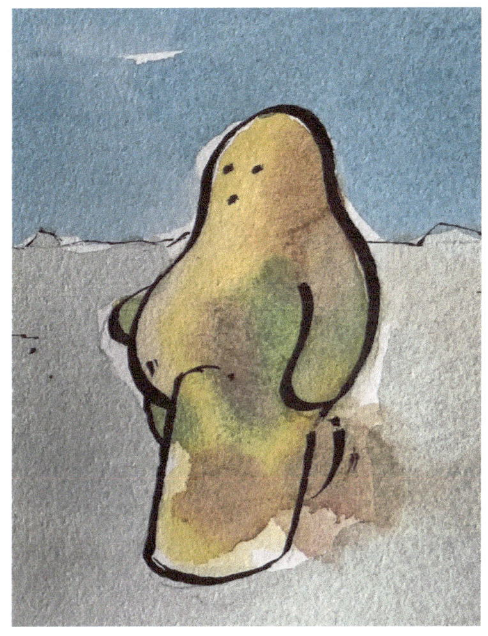

Joe Pascoe lives in Ivanhoe, Melbourne, with his family Lyndel, Eve and John. He has an Art History degree from La Trobe University and was a founding graduate in Museum Studies from Prahran CAE, which served him well throughout a long career in the visual arts.
Joe's other books of poetry are *Gum Tree Burning* (2019) and *Frangipani* (2020) Reading Sideways Press.

Don Walters is an Australian sculptor, painter and graphic artist. He has exhibited in Australia, Italy and France and has produced numerous public sculptures in Western Australia and Victoria. His work often incorporates cartoon-like characters into imagined landscapes and everyday situations. The artworks in this collaboration are from an ongoing series that began in France, moved to America and settled in Australia—all places where bubbles abound.

donwaltersart.com

in case of emergency press

We are proud to acknowledge the Traditional Owners of country throughout Australia
and to recognise their continuing connection to land, waters, and culture.

We pay our respects to their Elders past, present, and emerging.

We support recognition, reconciliation, and reparation.

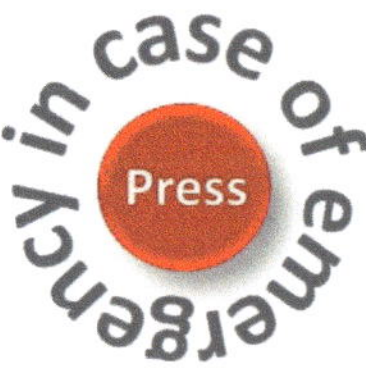